THE
ROMAN BATHS

A VIEW OVER 2000 YEARS

From the first century AD to the twentieth, people have been drawn to this place to seek comfort, cure and cleansing in the hot water that rises at its heart. What remains today is a remarkable sequence of ancient, medieval and later structures that give testimony to the continuous use of hot water here over nearly 2,000 years.

the Roman baths and temple of Aquae Sulis

the medieval King's Bath, heart of the complex

the Grand Pump Room, place of entertainment and refreshment

Antiquary and Archaeologist: the last 300 years

THE OFFICIAL GUIDE *by* BARRY CUNLIFFE

The origin of Bath

Bladud, the son of a British King, was a leper and for that reason was expelled from his father's palace. Becoming a swineherd, his pigs, were infected with the leprosy, but by rolling themselves in the warm mud through which they had to pass in their wanderings, they were soon cured. Bladud was eventually discovered taking his morning dip by two of the king's courtiers, who promptly took him home to his father. When he afterwards became king, he built the city of Bath B. C. 863 upon the muddy swamps which had proved so salutary to him.

The legendary origins of Bath as told on a postcard of 1908.

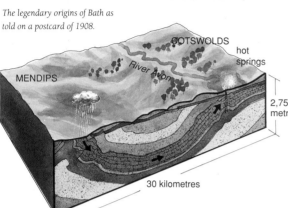

How the hot water reaches Bath: the probable passage through cave systems in the carboniferous limestone, where it acquires its heat at depth. The flow is driven by the high water table on Mendip. Analysis of the water's mineral content has revealed the different kinds of rock through which it has passed.

"Have you drank the waters, Mr Weller?" inquired his companion, as they walked towards High Street.

"Once," replied Sam.

"What did you think of 'em, Sir?"

"I thought they was particklery unpleasant," replied Sam.

"Ah," said Mr John Smauker, "you disliked the killibeate taste, perhaps?"

I don't know much about that 'ere," said Sam. "I thought they'd a wery strong flavour o'warm flat irons."

"That IS the killibeate, Mr Weller," observed Mr John Smauker, contemptuously.

THE PICKWICK PAPERS
Charles Dickens 1836

SPA WATER FACTS

RATE OF FLOW
13 litres per second or
1,106,400 litres (*c* 250,000 gallons) per day

TEMPERATURE
46°C (115°F)

MINERAL CONTENT
● there are 43 minerals in the water
● calcium and sulphate are the main dissolved ions; with sodium and chloride also important
● the water is low in dissolved metals except for iron which causes the orange staining
● the bubbling in the King's Bath is caused by exsolved gases escaping

COLOUR
The water is colourless but acquires its distinctive green hue from algae growth caused by its heat and daylight.

DRINKING THE WATER
Spa water may be tasted in the Pump Room. It is drawn up through a borehole sunk below the King's Bath.

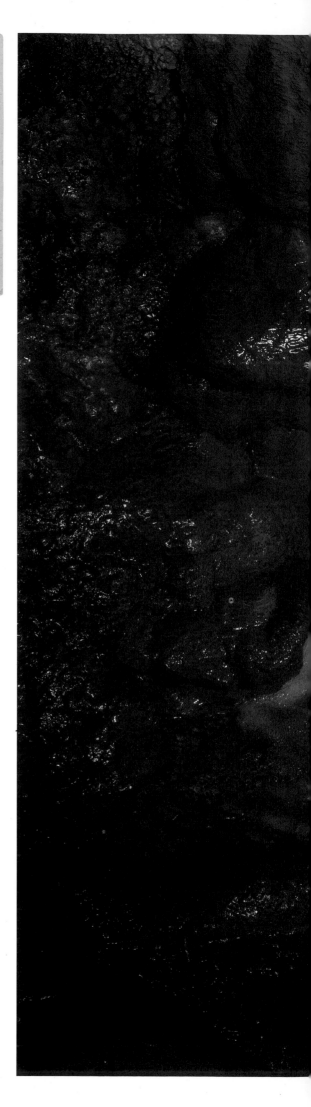

THE HOT SPRING

The continuous gush of hot mineral water which bursts from the ground in the centre of Bath has always been a subject of wonder. Imagine the scene 2000 years ago before the Romans came to tame the natural flow – a bubbling pool of murky green, hot to the touch, overflowing in a narrow stream to the river – the stream and pool fringed red with iron salts and everything overhung, on cold winters' days, with a pall of wisping steam. Little wonder that men believed the gods presided here. It was a liminal spot - an in-between place - where the realm of the earth and water deities communicated with our world and like all liminal space in the ancient world, it was dangerous. Even now, watching the water cascade from the Roman reservoir into the overflow drain, it is easy to forget time and place, our attention captured by the miracle of the waters.

Modern research explains it all, yet the fascination remains. The water we are watching now was, 10,000 years ago, rain falling on the Mendips. It percolated down through the carboniferous limestone deep into the earth where, between 2700-4300 m, natural heat raised the temperature to 64-96°C. The heated water then rose along fissures and faults through the limestone to the surface but lay trapped beneath impermeable layers of Lias clay until a fault could give access to the surface. That fault lies beneath Bath and allows a quarter of a million gallons of water a day to bubble free.

Mesolithic flint blades (actual size) found in the hot spring indicate that as early as 5,000 BC semi-nomadic bands of food-gatherers were attracted to the hot water.

3

Eighteen silver Celtic coins have been found in the Sacred Spring. Most of them are coins of the local tribe the Dobunni and some display their characteristic stylised horse with its tail in three strands.

By the first century BC this part of Britain was ruled by a Celtic tribe called the Dobunni. They believed that the spring was sacred to the goddess Sulis who, in common with many Celtic goddesses of rivers and springs, was probably thought to possess curative powers. At the spring it was possible to communicate with the underworld through the religious caste – the Druids – but the goddess would first have to be placated with offerings.

It was at about this time that the first recognised modifications were made to the spring. To reach the centre where the water bubbled up, a causeway of gravel and boulders was built out across the mud. Along here the worshippers, or more likely their religious intermediaries, walked so that their offerings of coins could be thrown into the potent centre.

In AD 43 the Roman armies landed in Kent to begin their relentless task of conquering Britain. The initial aim of the Emperor Claudius was to conquer only the productive and more civilised south-east, protecting the new province by a wide military zone stretching across the country from Exeter to Lincoln. For much of its length the frontier zone ran along the ridge of Jurassic hills (Cotswold and Northamptonshire Uplands) and was served by a military road now known as the Fosse Way. At intervals along the road, particularly where there were crossings, forts were built. One of these probably lay in or near Bath, though proof of its location has yet to be found.

For the Dobunni the Roman invasion brought dramatic change. Early in the year AD 43 the great spring festivals would have been celebrated in the time-honoured manner. By the next year most of their land was occupied by the alien Roman force and this most sacred site, the spring of Sulis, had been swallowed up within a heavily patrolled military zone.

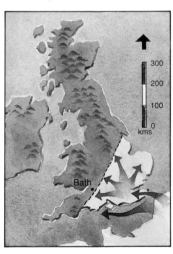

The Fosse Way military road serving the frontier zone crossed the river Avon in or near Bath. Between AD 43 and 47 the Romans subdued the south and east of England. From the earliest years of the occupation Bath lay at the interface of the Celtic and Roman worlds.

Sestertius of the emperor Vespasian (AD 69-79) from the Sacred Spring. Coins of Nero (AD 54-68) and Vespasian are the earliest to be thrown into the spring in large numbers, supporting the view that the baths and temple were built during the 60s and 70s.

The Romans were by no means insensitive to the gods and goddesses of those they conquered. These native deities were powerful forces who demanded respect. It was only the powerful Druids with their human sacrifices and, more worrying, their ability to stir up trouble for the Romans, who had to be annihilated. Thus Sulis and her spring remained while the landscape around them began to change.

We know little yet about the early years of Roman Bath. The fort, wherever it lies, is unlikely to have been in use for more than a few years before the army advanced into the West Midlands and South Wales. But during this time there can be little doubt that the soldiers learned of the power of the goddess: many would have paid their respects and some may have used the curative hot waters for bathing.

In the decade from about AD 50-60 the crossroads which grew up at the river crossing attracted traders and artisans, mostly native people but including perhaps a few retired soldiers, who settled on the outskirts of the sanctuary.

In AD 60 and the following year a devastating rebellion broke out led by the British queen Boudica. Many thousands were killed and the revenge of the Roman military was uncontrolled in its violence. By the end of the episode the province lay in ruins. It took ten years to repair the physical, psychological and political damage that had been done in the few months of fury.

It was probably during this period of reconstruction that the Roman authorities took the decision to turn the native sanctuary of Sulis into a magnificent curative establishment – perhaps a symbol of reconciliation. Work began by enclosing the spring within a massive reservoir wall lined with sheets of lead, the unstable ground around consolidated with driven piles of oak. Only when the spring was tamed could work begin on the construction of a temple and a suite of luxurious baths.

The open reservoir containing the hot spring lay at the heart of the new complex. Its practical function was to the south – it provided a head of spa water for the curative baths. Its religious function was to the north – it lay within the temple precinct where worshippers could approach it to make their offering to the presiding Sulis Minerva.

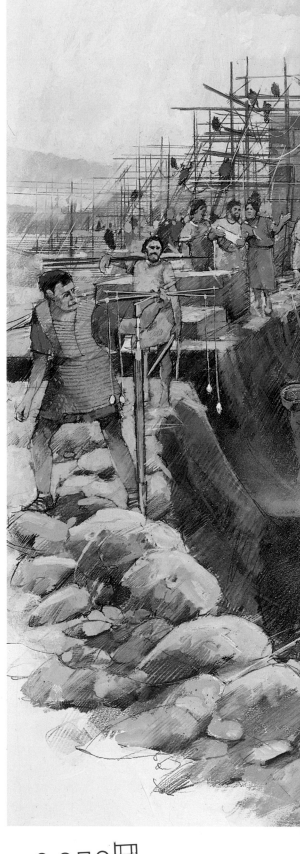

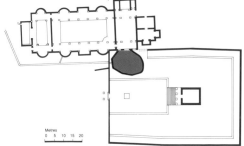

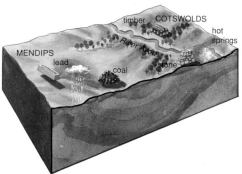

Controlling the spring and building around it required large quantities of raw materials. Timber for piling, scaffolding and roofing would have been felled locally; oolitic limestone for building was quarried from the downs overlooking the site; lead to line the reservoir, baths and channels was extracted from the Mendip Hills; and coal for stoking furnaces and burning in the temple came from the north Somerset coalfield to the south.

7

BATH AND THE EMPIRE

The Porta Nigra at Trier, one of the principal towns of eastern Gaul. It was from here that Peregrinus came to erect his altar in the temple precinct at Bath. His name meaning 'the wanderer' seems to be quite appropriate.

PEREGRINUS SON OF SECUNDUS, A TREVERAN, TO LOUCETIUS MARS AND NEMETONA WILLINGLY AND DESERVEDLY FULFILLED HIS VOW

Reverse of a bronze as of Hadrian (AD 117-138) showing the seated figure of Britannia. Numerous such coins, all corroded by the mineral water, have been found in the Sacred Spring.

BATH

LONDON

ROME

JULIUS VITALIS ARMOURER OF THE TWENTIETH LEGION VALERIA VICTRIX, OF 9 YEARS SERVICE, AGED 29, A BELGIC TRIBESMAN, WITH FUNERAL AT THE COST OF THE GUILD OF ARMOURERS: HE LIES HERE

LUCIUS VITELLIUS TANCINUS, SON OF MANTAIUS, A TRIBESMAN OF CAURIUM IN SPAIN, TROOPER OF THE CAVALRY REGIMENT OF VETTONES. ROMAN CITIZEN, AGED 46, OF 26 YEARS SERVICE LIES BURIED HERE

The province of Britannia lay on the edge of the civilised world and by no means all of the tribes of the islands were conquered. Wales remained largely under military control throughout, large areas of north and west Scotland remained beyond the frontiers and no Roman troops ever set foot in Ireland. Britannia, then, was a frontier province and, away from the civilised south-east with its capital at Londinium, even the towns would have had a distinctly rustic air. Foreign soldiers, administrators and entrepreneurs flooded into the province but the bulk of the population, even those who became officials in the towns and lived in villas adorned with mosaics, were native Britons.

Rome imposed on Britain not only its administrative systems, including taxes to be paid to the central government, but also its own sense of values. The historian Tacitus, writing of the governor Agricola in the 80s of the first century said that he gave official encouragement to the building of temples, public squares and good houses in the knowledge that the desire for such attributes of 'civilisation' would be a sure way to encourage the native population to accept Roman rule. It was in this spirit of enthusiasm to embrace the visible signs of Roman culture that the great sanctuary developed at Bath.

Its fame spread rapidly, no doubt at first among the soldiers who were stationed here in the early years. Some later returned to retire or simply to pay a short visit to take a cure.

Some died in Bath, remembered only in their tombstones. Gradually news of the curative establishment spread to the Continent and so the trickle of visitors grew, some of them commemorating their visits with altars set up to the local deities.

In the second century the Greek geographers named Bath as *Aquae Calidae* – the Hot Waters – but it seems to have become more widely known as *Aquae Sulis* – the Waters of Sulis – appropriately commemorating the presiding goddess.

Inscribed tombstones and altars record people from different parts of the Empire being at Bath. Lucius Vitellius Tancinus served in a cavalry unit raised in Spain while Gaius Murrius of the 2nd legion Adiutrix came from Fréjus in southern France. While soldiers had no say in their postings to Britain, civilians chose to come here. Priscus, a stonemason from Chartres, may have sought work here while Rusonia Aventina from Metz and Peregrinus from Trier may have come here to seek a cure. Coins from the Eastern Empire, such as the tetradrachm of Elagabalus (AD 218-222) minted at Antioch, could not be spent in the West and may have been thrown into the Sacred Spring by well-travelled pilgrims.

Some visitors to Bath are not recorded by name, but fragments from their mausoleums recovered from cemeteries outside the town still contain useful information about the people they represent. The colossal head commemorating a wealthy lady can be dated by her hairstyle to the late first century. This tells us that only fifty years after the Roman invasion rich people, civilians including women were to be found at Bath.

THE TEMPLE BUILDINGS

The temple of Sulis Minerva was decorated with elaborately carved cornices, the work of skilled craftsmen. The abundance of local limestone would have provided material for a local sculptor Sulinus, who also had a workshop in Cirencester. His other work would have included altars, tombs and domestic sculptures.

The arrangement of the sanctuary was both elegant and logical. The focal point was, of course, the spring now contained within a large open reservoir. To the north stood the temple, set, together with the reservoir, within an open precinct while to the south were built the curative baths fed by the hot waters.

The temple, in its original late first-century form, was a purely classical building set high on a podium reached by a steep flight of steps. Its

porch was dominated by four massive fluted columns with foliate Corinthian capitals supporting a triangular pediment. Behind lay a simple room – the cella – where the cult statue and sacred objects were kept. The temple faced a paved yard towards the centre of which was the sacrificial altar, so sited as to be on the east-west axis through the temple and the north-south axis across the spring.

Gradually modifications were made to this simple arrangement, the most dramatic coming in the second century when the Sacred Spring was enclosed in a massive vaulted chamber. The only access to the waters was through a small door opposite the altar or by means of three large openings from the baths to the south. At the same time the temple podium was extended to create an ambulatory around it and the steps were flanked by small shrines.

Later the north wall of the reservoir hall began to tip outwards under the weight of the vault. This required massive buttressing cleverly disguised in an ornamental style with the central buttress taking the form of a *quadrifrons*, a two-way arch. To balance this a new building decorated with cupids and the four seasons was built on the north side of the altar. Carved blocks from this structure have been found but its exact position is not known.

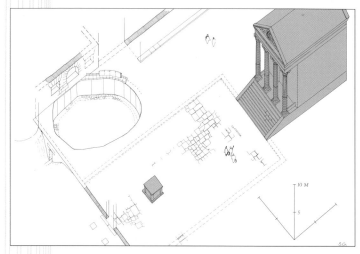

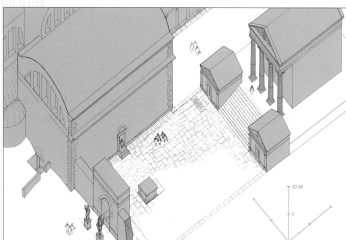

Some Roman temples still stand today, such as the Maison Carrée (above left) at Nimes in Southern Gaul, erected in AD 2-3. Two or three generations later, classically trained craftsmen from Gaul may well have come to work on the temple in Bath.

TO THE SULEVIAE
SULINUS,
A SCULPTOR, SON
OF BRUCETUS,
GLADLY AND
DESERVEDLY MADE
THIS OFFERING

SACRIFICE AND CEREMONY

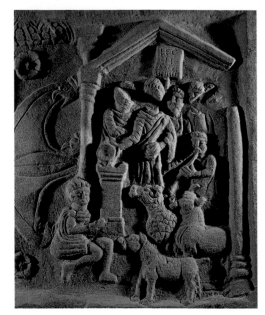

Relief carving from the Antonine Wall. A sacrifice is about to take place in front of a temple; libations are poured onto a small altar, pipes are played and unsuspecting sheep look on. Similar altars have been found on the temple precinct.

Inscribed block recording Lucius Marcius Memor, the haruspex.

Unlike the modern church or mosque where participants in the religious ceremony congregate inside the building, in Roman religious observances the rituals generally took place outside in the precinct around the large sacrificial altar. In Bath the paved area upon which the altar stood provided ample space for those who wished to participate.

Public ceremonies usually involved the sacrifice of an animal to the deity. In those cases where the endowment was sufficient to allow it, a cow, a sheep and a pig might be slaughtered together.

One of the most important functionaries on those occasions was the augur (*haruspex*). His task was to examine the entrails of the sacrificed beast, particularly the liver, for marks or blemishes from which he could foretell the future. If the sacrifice was taking place in advance of a proposed enterprise, inauspicious marks on the liver would be seen as an omen from the deity indicating that the venture be postponed.

By remarkable good fortune an inscribed stone pedestal was found close to the altar. It tells us that Lucius Marcius Memor, a *haruspex*, made a dedication to the goddess Sulis, the item dedicated presumably being a statue originally standing on the base. This is the only recorded instance of an augur in Britain.

In addition to the great sacrificial altar the precinct would have been cluttered with a number of smaller altars to the deity set up by private individuals in anticipation of a divine favour or in thanks for having received one. These stones were always inscribed with the names of the donors. Decked with flowers or supporting containers of smouldering incense, they would have added a vivid dimension to the sanctuary.

One of the altar cornerstones has been discovered built into the church of St Mary at Compton Dando. The stone can be seen at the base of the right-hand buttress. In the medieval period Compton Dando belonged to the Bath monastery estates which may account for the stone's presence.

Tin mask, probably used in temple ceremonies. The eye recesses may have housed precious stones. Holes around the edge suggest that it was mounted on a wooden frame.
A priest, concealed by his hood and a mask, would make an imposing sight at a ceremony.

Two corner blocks of the sacrificial altar. Both stand on the altar platform in the temple precinct. One is decorated with reliefs of Hercules Bibax and Jupiter, the other with Bacchus and a unidentified female figure.

In Britain are many great rivers, and warm springs adorned with sumptuous splendour for the use of mortals. Minerva is the patron goddess of these and in her temple the eternal flames never whiten into ash, but rather, when the fire dies away, it turns into round rocky masses.

Solinus 3rd c AD

One of the most dramatic discoveries ever made in Bath was of the life-size gilded bronze head of Minerva. It was found in 1727 by workmen digging a sewer deep beneath Stall Street. The head was from the cult statue which would have been housed in the *cella* of the temple. Originally she would have worn a tall Corinthian helmet – a sign of her martial prowess.

At first sight, so classical an image might seem out of place at a spring dedicated to the Celtic water deity Sulis but the Romans were pragmatic people. Faced with a spring sacred to Sulis they would have enquired of her attributes and hearing, no doubt, that she was renowned for healing, for wisdom and perhaps for military insight they would have decided that Sulis was none other than their own Minerva. Thereafter the two names were interchangeable and we often find the deity called Sulis Minerva on inscriptions. Such conflations were common in the Roman provinces. They satisfied native susceptibilities, made otherwise obscure local cults immediately intelligible to visitors and gave reassurance to those who believed in the universality of the classical pantheon.

In iconography it would have been conventional to allude to Sulis Minerva's various attributes – weapons for her martial powers and the owl for her wisdom. The rather more obscure symbolism on the temple pediment and the very incomplete pediment of the quadrifrons seem to refer to water and the sun. Her power over the spring is self-evident. It may be that in her Celtic guise Sulis was also in some way connected with the sun as one interpretation of her name (Sul = sol = sun) might imply.

Bust of Minerva in the British Museum, complete with helmet. Even without the helmet the Bath head was recognisable as Minerva.

THE GODDESS SULIS MINERVA

Inscriptions reveal that the Celtic and Roman deities were considered one and the same. Several *paterae* or libation vessels excavated from the Sacred Spring bear the legend *deae Suli Minervae* - "to the goddess Sulis Minerva". Two stone altars from the other hot springs nearby carry the same dedication, one made by Sulinus, son of Maturus - perhaps a local man - the other by Gaius Curiatius Saturninus, Centurion of the Second Legion Augusta, perhaps visiting Bath from his base at Caerleon in South Wales

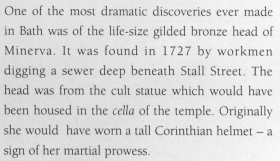

Silver patera handle with gilded detail from Capheaton, Northumberland, showing similarities with the cult at Bath. Minerva stands holding her spear and shield while below a worshipper makes an offering at an altar in front of a temple. Below the temple a spring is pouring from a hole in the ground. Male and female water gods flank the scene, reminiscent of the tritons in the corners of the temple pediment.

Reverse of a copper alloy coin from the Sacred Spring bearing the figure of the goddess Minerva. This would have been thought a particularly suitable offering to make.

THE TEMPLE PEDIMENT

The Gorgon's head image resembles other gods associated with water, such as the face of Oceanus at the centre of a large circular silver dish from Mildenhall, Suffolk.

A Gorgon's head can be seen on the breastplate of this relief carving of Minerva found in the Roman Baths.

The elaborately carved pediment of the temple is redolent with meaning of Celtic and Roman significance – if only we could interpret it!

The general layout is clear enough. Dominating everything is a large roundel, probably a shield, bearing a head with fearsome flowing hair, and held aloft by two winged Victories. Creatures called tritons neatly fit the awkward triangular corners and immediately below the shield are two helmets, one with an owl perched on it.

The helmets and owl are clear references to Minerva's attributes of military prowess and wisdom. So, at least superficially, is the head on the shield if it is interpreted as the Gorgon's head cut off by Perseus and carried thus so that those who saw it would be turned to stone. Minerva is frequently shown with a shield of this kind. But there are difficulties, for the head, though closely similar to the female Gorgon, is blatantly male and in his flowing hair and wings there are clear similarities to the sea gods Oceanus or Neptune, an allusion further echoed by the tritons. But if the hair is regarded as flaming and the small star above is significant here perhaps is also a reference to the sun god Sol!

These are difficult matters for us to penetrate, just as modern Christian iconography would be puzzling in the extreme to a Roman. Perhaps what the sculptor was doing was to give us deliberately enigmatic glimpses of the many powers and forms of the presiding deity. The fleeting visions changing shape as one looked up at them would have been entirely familiar to the Celt used to his gods constantly shape-shifting. The Bath pediment, like the sanctuary it dominated, is a brilliant evocation of the fusion of Celt and Roman.

OTHER GODS

During its development the sanctuary acquired many additional monuments and some new buildings. Among the most interesting was the two-way arch (the *quadrifrons*) which served as a buttress to the wall of the reservoir hall, and the elaborately sculptured monument known as the Facade of the Four Seasons which faced it. The pediment of the quadrifrons was carved with two figures, standing either side of a rock from which water pours, holding aloft a roundel bearing a head with a spike crown. This was almost certainly the sun god Sol, his postion above the gushing water alluding no doubt to the hot spring rising immediately beyond him.

The pediment of the Facade of the Four Seasons is more complete and depicts the goddess Luna holding her riding whip as she rides her chariot across the night sky. The symbolism of the two is beautifully balanced, Luna commanding the dark northern hemisphere and Sol the light south - female:male, north:south, dark:light, cold:hot. And rising dominant over both – the pediment of Sulis Minerva's temple.

One further building deserves attention. There exist a series of stone blocks, found in the nineteenth century, which are clearly part of a circular temple (a *tholos*) of exactly the same width as the main temple. Where it stood we can only guess, but from the position where the pieces were found it probably lay to the east of the main precinct and its foundations may now be under the front of the Abbey. Circular temples of this kind are exceedingly rare in the western Roman provinces since the idea was essentially Greek. Could it be that the Emperor Hadrian – who loved Greek culture – set up the *tholos* at Bath when he visited the province in the early second century? The idea is attractive but must remain at present unproven. The *tholos* is still very much a mystery.

This altar, found on the temple precinct in 1753, suggests that at some point the temple of Sulis Minerva suffered desecration 'by insolent hands'. The sponsor of the repairs thought it fitting to dedicate his good works to the divinity of the emperor.

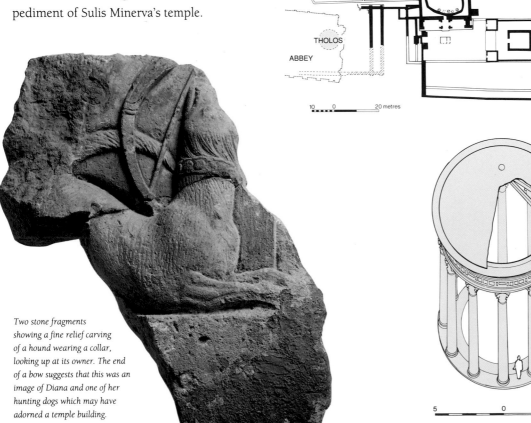

Two stone fragments showing a fine relief carving of a hound wearing a collar, looking up at its owner. The end of a bow suggests that this was an image of Diana and one of her hunting dogs which may have adorned a temple building.

The likely presence of a tholos opposite the temple of Sulis Minerva supports evidence from elsewhere in the centre of Bath that Aquae Sulis was not a normal Roman town but a temenos or sanctuary containing shrines, baths and public buildings.

18

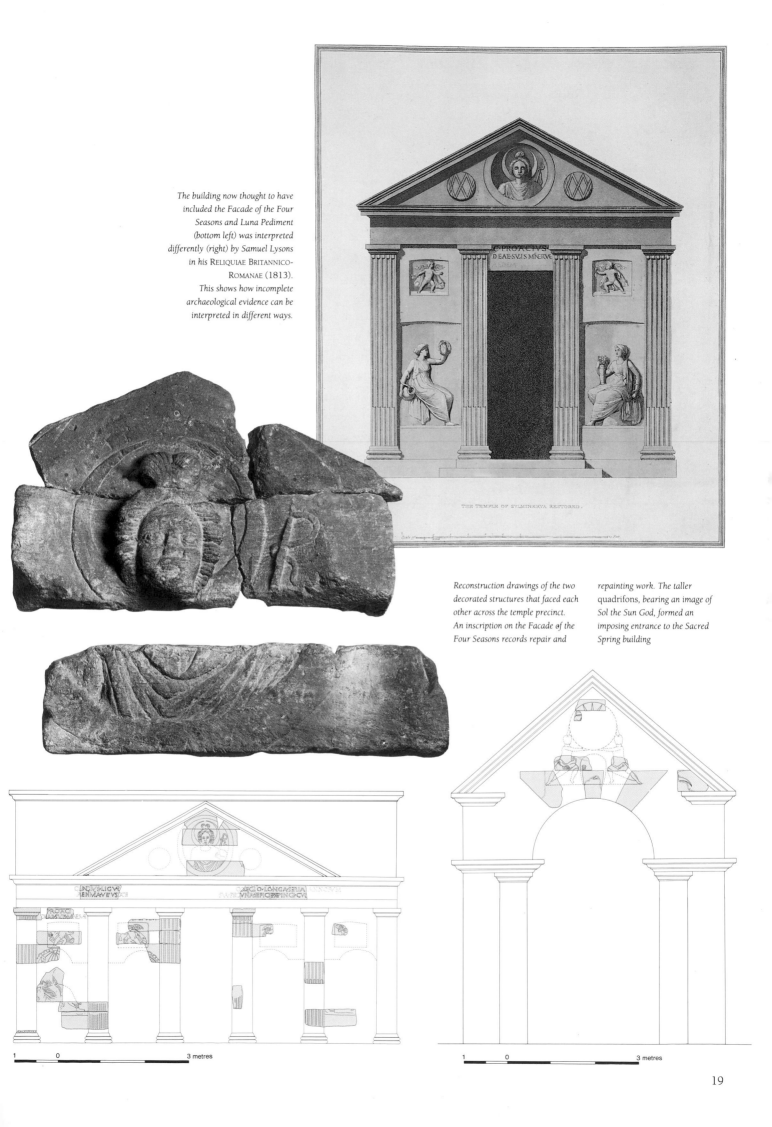

The building now thought to have included the Facade of the Four Seasons and Luna Pediment (bottom left) was interpreted differently (right) by Samuel Lysons in his RELIQUIAE BRITANNICO-ROMANAE (1813). This shows how incomplete archaeological evidence can be interpreted in different ways.

Reconstruction drawings of the two decorated structures that faced each other across the temple precinct. An inscription on the Facade of the Four Seasons records repair and repainting work. The taller quadrifons, bearing an image of Sol the Sun God, formed an imposing entrance to the Sacred Spring building

1   0   3 metres

1   0   3 metres

THE HEALING SPRING

The spring was the point at which our world could communicate with the deity. Those requiring divine intervention made their wishes known to the goddess, by performing a sacrifice or making a gift in anticipation of a successful outcome.

One way to ensure that the goddess knew what was required was to have the message inscribed on a sheet of lead or pewter which was then thrown into the spring. Like all legal documents it was important to get the wording exactly right and this may have involved the use of trained scribes. A number of these messages have been recovered from the spring. For the most part they are curses inviting the deity to punish a wrongdoer, someone who may have stolen a bath robe or a few *denarii*. Usually the person placing the curse did not know exactly who it was but was able to provide a list of suspects. If the culprit were named, the goddess would know and could act. The threat of divine wrath would be a powerful deterrent.

The spring was also a place where gifts were made to the goddess. Excavation has brought to light thousands of coins, items of jewellery and a collection of pewter and silver dishes and handled cups (*paterae*), usually inscribed with a dedication to Sulis Minerva. These *paterae* raise the question of the use of the water. Was it drunk or poured to provide a cure? We will never know but we can be sure that the immersion of the body in the spring water, in the bathing establishment, was thought to have curative value. It was also believed in the ancient world that just being in the temple or sleeping there would allow healing powers of the gods to work.

The temple must have been thronged with hangers-on – the scribes writing the curses, the sellers of religious trinkets and the oculist whose stamp was found in Abbey Yard in 1731 selling his concoctions to cure eye disease. Wherever there are people hoping to be cured, there are the unscrupulous who will prey on their frailty.

Artist's impression of the Sacred Spring. No bathing would take place here. Visitors could enter through a doorway from the temple precinct, while three arched openings opposite gave people in the baths a view of the spring. Large numbers of coins were found immediately below the openings.

Lead curse found in the Sacred Spring in 1879. Romantic interpretations have suggested that Vilbia was a girl taken from her lover, but a re-examination of this otherwise unknown name points to a more mundane possession, such as a napkin, being stolen. The aggrieved complainant, unsure of whom to blame, offered the goddess a list of likely culprits.

Candle holder in the form of a stag, one of a number of pewter objects found in the spring in 1878-9. Pewter was manufactured near Bath in the later Roman period and these items may have been made specifically for use at the temple.

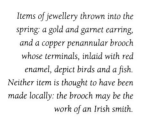

Items of jewellery thrown into the spring: a gold and garnet earring, and a copper penannular brooch whose terminals, inlaid with red enamel, depict birds and a fish. Neither item is thought to have been made locally: the brooch may be the work of an Irish smith.

Some of the thirty-four late 1st century intaglios found in the drain, washed from either the spring or the baths. The collection may have been

the offering of a gem-cutter; alternatively they may have been lost from finger rings in the baths.

Ivory breasts carved from a roundel of tusk. Model organs or limbs were offered at sacred sites as petitions – or thanks – for a cure.

The votives cast into the Spring varied greatly, ranging from large pewter ewers through smaller libation vessels to the many thousands of coins. Some 1st century coins were found in almost mint condition, perhaps offerings made by soldiers or administrators whose pay had only recently arrived in Britain. Most of the coins are copper alloy, many badly corroded by the mineral water; some are silver and a few are gold.

CONTROLLING THE WATER

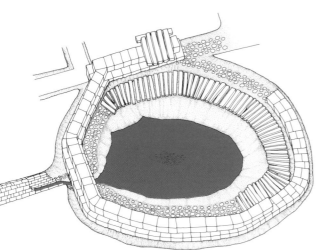

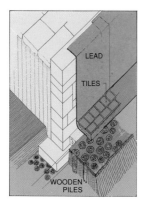

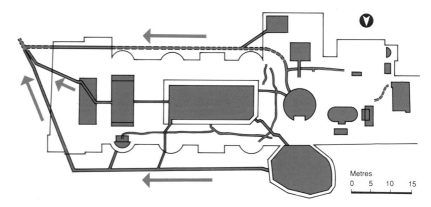

The stone reservoir in which the hot water rises and the channels that conduct it through the baths still function as the Roman engineers intended them to. Some parts were purely functional and not meant to be seen; others, like the overflow arch from the spring, were clearly intended to impress the viewer.

The Roman baths are a masterpiece of civil engineering. Not only is their architecture highly effective in its elegant simplicity, the delicate hydraulic engineering controlling the water flow shows a detailed knowledge of the art of taming springs.

The main spring was enclosed by a reservoir wall 2m high internally lined with lead to prevent leakage. The reservoir performed two functions – it provided a head of water to feed the great lead-lined swimming bath and its subsidiary pools, and it served as a settling tank to retain the volumes of sand brought up by the force of the spring and prevent the sediment from blocking the narrow culvert and pipes. After a while the reservoir itself would have begun to silt up but the problem was easily overcome by opening a sluice towards the base of the reservoir wall, allowing the force of the water to wash the sand out through a man-sized overflow drain.

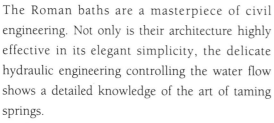

A lead pipe, still in situ today, took hot water from the spring to a fountain halfway down the Great Bath. It also supplied a small immersion pool in the East Baths. Pipes were made by hammering sheet lead around a wooden pole and then sweating the joint to make them watertight.

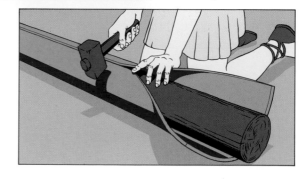

CONTROLLING THE WATER

The hot spring water flowed constantly into the Great Bath through a lead box culvert at its north-western corner, as it does today. Some water passed to other baths at the east end but the excess was taken away through a sluice-controlled drain in the north-east corner and fed into the main overflow drain. The system was simple but highly effective, the constant flow keeping the baths hot and the drains clear.

Later in the life of the baths modifications were made and additional plumbing was needed to serve the new installations. The most evident today is a length of Roman lead pipe set into the paving on the north side of the Great Bath. It was to take a constant supply of water to a fountain in the form of a reclining water god (now almost unrecognizable through weathering) in the centre of the north side of the bath.

The hot water may have flowed into the Great Bath under a stone slab bearing a dedication to the presiding deity.

The Great Bath, like some modern spa pools, has a flat bottom and steps on all four sides. The bottom is still lined with forty five sheets of Mendip lead laid to prevent cold ground water from cooling the bath. The raised joints between the lead sheets are clearly visible. When filled the bath is 1.5m (5 feet) deep.

ROMAN BATHING

One of the late Roman emperors was asked by an incredulous barbarian chieftain why he bathed once a day. The emperor answered in apologetic innocence that it was because he was now too busy to bathe twice. Bathing was extremely important in Roman society.

The baths provided a context for social interaction to take place. By the number of his attendants and the fragrance and quality of the oils with which he was massaged a man could demonstrate his social status. There he would also be prepared to receive his clients to discuss business, again impressing others with his importance. In the baths one could debate the issues of the day sitting in the alcoves away from splashing from the pool, or listen to the discourses of philosophers. Most establishments also had courts for games and exercise where the body could be tired before taking the sauna or Turkish treatment, finishing with a quick dip in the cold pool.

Mixed bathing in public was not uncommon at first but in the more prudish times of the second century the Emperor Hadrian passed a law forbidding it. Thereafter baths had different opening hours for males and females but some establishments, of which Bath seems to have been one, built additional facilities so that both sexes could be accommodated at the same time.

No doubt the bathing establishment here would have functioned like any normal town baths but in addition it was curative. People came here to immerse themselves in the health-giving waters. It is for this reason that large swimming pools, rare in normal urban baths, are such a dominant feature of the baths of Bath.

The Baths of Caracalla by Sir Lawrence Alma-Tadema (1836-1912), a high Victorian vision of the opulent baths of ancient Rome. The trio of winsome maidens seem oblivious to the antics of the bathers behind them. The baths of Aquae Sulis, although curative in function, also offered the chance to relax and talk in the passages and alcoves around the Great Bath.

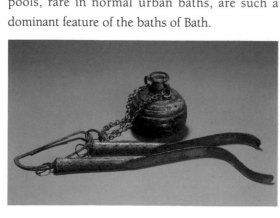

Bathing set of strigils and oil flask from the British Museum. This would be a common set of personal equipment, much like a sponge bag today. In the hottest of the hypocaust rooms the bather would massage scented oil into the body then scrape down with the sharp strigil. This would remove the oil, sweat, dirt and hair from the skin.

DEVELOPMENT OF THE BATHS

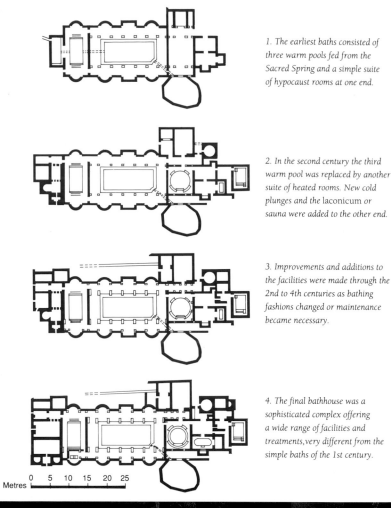

1. The earliest baths consisted of three warm pools fed from the Sacred Spring and a simple suite of hypocaust rooms at one end.

When the baths were built in the late first century AD they were elegant in their simplicity. You entered a massive hall with a dramatic view of the Sacred Spring through three openings in the north wall. From here you could take a normal bath, going first into the *tepidarium* (warm room) and then the *caldarium* (hot room) before jumping into a cold plunge at the south end of the hall. Or you could opt first to swim in the three pools of the curative establishment.

As time went on so the facilities were increased. First the west baths were provided with a *laconicum* – a circular room offering an intensely hot dry atmosphere like a sauna – and a new cold plunge was inserted into the old entrance hall. At about the same time a completely new suite of baths was added at the east end.

2. In the second century the third warm pool was replaced by another suite of heated rooms. New cold plunges and the laconicum or sauna were added to the other end.

3. Improvements and additions to the facilities were made through the 2nd to 4th centuries as bathing fashions changed or maintenance became necessary.

4. The final bathhouse was a sophisticated complex offering a wide range of facilities and treatments, very different from the simple baths of the 1st century.

Metres 0 5 10 15 20 25

Bathers would complete their visit to the heated rooms by taking a cold plunge to rinse off, freshen up and close the pores of their skin. While there was an endless supply of hot water on site, cold water would have to be ducted in from springs or wells elsewhere.

Tiles were used extensively in roofs. Box tiles were used in the vaults, being light, strong and an insulating layer. Surfaces were combed before firing to help mortar and plaster adhere. Sometimes stray animals in the tile works would step in unfired clay and have their imprint preserved!

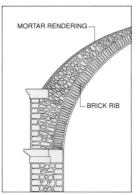

MORTAR RENDERING

BRICK RIB

The use of lime rubble mortar enabled the Romans to construct ambitious roof structures. Timber formwork would be erected and the tile and mortar roof laid over it. When the mortar had set the formwork would be removed.

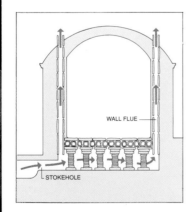

WALL FLUE

STOKEHOLE

Hypocausts were used to heat the tepidarium and calidarium. Furnaces directed hot air below the rooms, heating the brick pillars and the undersides of the floors. The hot air escaped to chimneys through flues in the walls. Few would ever see the hypocausts except the unfortunates charged with clearing them of soot.

The most dramatic change came in the middle or late second century when the timber roofs of the Great Bath and entrance hall (now containing the circular bath) were removed, quite possibly because they had started to warp or rot. The walls and piers were then strengthened to support new vaults of tile and concrete flung with assurance across these considerable spaces. Reroofing on this scale was a remarkable engineering achievement.

Thereafter the baths continued to be modified and extended. Nowhere is this more apparent than at the east end where the different floor levels can be seen today. In a final stage it seems that the hypocaust (underfloor heating) systems had begun to be susceptible to flooding and it was necessary to raise all the floor levels.

The baths today are a remarkable monument to the skill of the Roman engineers who built and maintained them over more than three centuries of public service.

BATHING FACILITIES

The suite of baths at the western end of the complex grew from a simple pair of hypocaust rooms in the first century AD into a complicated building offering a number of cleansing facilities. In addition to the Turkish style wet-heat rooms bathers could make use of cold water plunges, more popular as medical treatment in the later

Empire, and a small circular laconicum or dry-heat sauna. Careful planning was required to ensure that wet-heat and dry-heat facilities were kept well apart and that service areas such as hypocaust stokeries and storage yards for fuel were separate from public areas used by bathers.

The circular pool, installed in the second century as part of the expanding facilities, occupied the original unheated entrance hall. This lay on a significant alignment, the north-south axis of the site, which passed through the Sacred Spring and sacrificial altar immediately to the north. The ability to see across the Sacred Spring to the temple precinct was a reminder to bathers of the religious nature of the site.

COLLAPSE OF THE EMPIRE

Two gold aureii of the British usurper Allectus (AD 293-296) thrown into the Sacred Spring, probably by a well paid official. Very few others of this denomination are known.

Late in the third century the scene was finally set for the disintegration of the Roman empire – a process which was to take a hundred and fifty years. Barbarians from beyond the frontiers broke through in a series of devastating raids, usurpers set themselves up as emperors, manpower declined and the economy began to fragment. There was no one reason why the empire collapsed – it was an inevitable downward spiral intensified by widespread disillusionment.

Against this background Britain fared quite well. As an island it was conveniently isolated from the barbarian inroads of the late third century and though it was ruled by usurpers as a breakaway province for a while, by the early fourth century, when central authority had been re-established, there is ample evidence of real prosperity especially in the countryside where estate owners began to build luxurious villas adorned with fine mosaics.

For Britain the end began in 367 when a concerted attack was made on the province by barbarians from all sides. The Bath region seems to have suffered. Villas were destroyed and the slaughtered inhabitants thrown down wells. Within a few years some semblance of stability was restored for a decade or two but in the face of

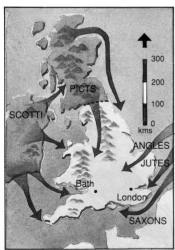

The island province of Britannia faced many barbarian attacks from the sea. Coastal defences were built and towns raised local militias or engaged Germanic mercenaries to help them.

The barbarians drive us to the sea and the sea drives us back to the barbarians...

Among the innumerable monuments of architecture constructed by the Romans, how many have escaped the notice of history, how few have resisted the ravages of time and barbarism!...

THE DECLINE AND FALL OF
THE ROMAN EMPIRE
Edward Gibbon 1776-88

The baths of Hadrian's Villa, Tivoli, by Piranesi (1720-1778). The crumbling vaulted baths of Aquae Sulis must have looked very like this after their abandonment. Swamps caused by the flooding spring and uncontrolled vegetation would have made the standing remains quite inaccessible. Excavations in the 1880s found a wildfowl's nest and egg in the post-Roman swamp levels in the baths.

increasing barbarian raids and immigration and the general disintegration of the authority of the empire, the province of Britannia dissolved into a confusion of warring factions. Populations fled from the cities and no longer was there the will or the ability to maintain the urban infrastructure.

In Bath the baths and the temple became increasingly derelict. The drainage system broke down and extensive flooding began. For a while tips of rubble were laid from time to time in the temple precinct to consolidate the mud but eventually the rising water won and black mud covered everything.

Wondrous is this masonry, shattered by the Fates.

The fortifications have given way,

the buildings raised by giants are crumbling.

The roofs have collapsed; the towers are in ruins...

there is rime on the mortar.

The walls are rent and broken away

and have fallen undermined by age.

The owners and builders are perished and gone

and have been held fast in the Earth's embrace,

the ruthless clutch of the grave,

while a hundred generations of mankind have passed away..

Red of hue and hoary with lichen

this wall has outlasted kingdom after kingdom,

standing unmoved by storms.

The lofty arch has fallen...

resolute in spirit he marvellously clamped the foundations

of the walls with ties

there were splendid palaces and many halls with water

flowing through them

And so these courts lie desolate

and the framework of the dome with its red arches shed its tiles...

where of old many a warrior,

joyous hearted and radiant with gold,

shone resplendent in the harness of battle,

proud and flushed with wine.

He gazed upon the treasure, the silver, the precious stones,

upon wealth, riches and pearls,

upon this splendid citadel of a broad domain.

There stood courts of stone,

and a stream gushed forth in rippling floods of hot water.

The wall enfolded within its bright bosom

the whole place which contained the hot flood of the baths.........

'THE RUIN', an eighth
century poem probably
written by a monk at the
adjacent monastery,
inspired by the deserted,
crumbling remains
of the Roman temple
and baths. The poem is
incomplete and the site
is unnamed, but the
references to hot water
and the many structural
elements revealed by
archaeology leave little
doubt that the poet was
in Bath.

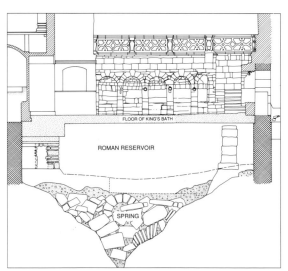

Streamlets of water, warmed without human agency and from the very bowels of the earth, (flow) into a receptacle beautifully constructed with chambered arches. These form baths in the middle of the city, warm and wholesome and charming to the eye. Sick persons from all over England resort thither to bathe in these healing waters and the fit also, to see these wonderful burstings out of warm water and to bathe in them.

Gesta Stephani c. 1133

The King's Bath shown as an inset on Speed's plan of Bath published in 1610. Niches on three sides provided seating for bathers while galleries above gave onlookers a good view of activity in the bath. The adjoining New or Queen's Bath was added in 1575 and was fed from the King's Bath.

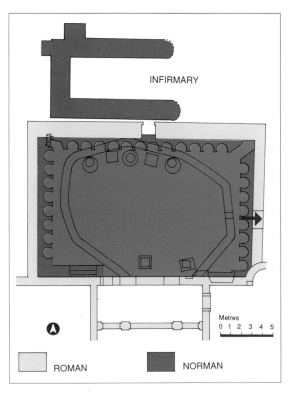

The Norman King's Bath was created using the surviving walls of the rectangular Roman Sacred Spring building. The bath's floor was laid over the debris in the spring. The monastic infirmary was built on the north side of the bath over the Roman temple precinct.

Section showing work of many periods now visible in the King's Bath. The spring contains collapsed Roman building material. Facing us are medieval niches with the 17th century balustrade over them. The wall on the right is Roman while opposite it stands the Pump Room.

...*The Kinges Bathe is very faire and large standing almost in the midle of the towne, and at the west end of the cathedrale chirch. ...The colour of the water of the baynes is as it were a depe blew se water, and rikth like a seting potte contiually, having sumwhat a sulphureus and sumwhat onpleasant savor.*

LELAND'S ITINERARY 1540

The emergence of Bath from the ruins of *Aquae Sulis* is a process still being actively researched by archaeologists but we can be reasonably sure that the ruins of the great Roman public buildings stood gaunt above the marsh and dereliction to serve as an awful reminder to people, like the author of 'The Ruin', of the transience of worldly power. But all this time the spring continued to flow, to serve as it always has done as a focus of attraction.

In 675, Osric, king of the Hwicce, a sub-kingdom of Mercia, granted estates to the Abbess Berta to endow a convent of Holy Virgins at Bath. More land was given a few years later and in 757-8 we hear of land being made over to the brothers of the monastic church of St. Peter in Bath. Whether, as it seems likely, these early ecclesiastical establishments clustered together in the centre of the town around the spring, it is impossible yet to say, but Saxon burials have been found just north of the spring within the old temple precinct and spreading over the east end of the baths.

The monastery flourished and in 781 could be called 'most famous': by the tenth century the church was said to be 'of wondrous workmanship' and it was here, in 973, that Edgar was crowned king of England in the presence of the Archbishops of York and Canterbury. Bath had by now regained something of its former glory.

The old Saxon monastery was eventually torn down and replaced by a fine new structure built by the Norman bishop John of Tours in the twelfth century. Appropriately the monastic infirmary was constructed over the temple precinct just north of the spring and the Roman walls of the hall which once enclosed the spring were utilized to create a new bath – henceforth known as the King's Bath – fed direct by the hot springs bubbling up through the tons of collapsed Roman masonry which clogged the reservoir.

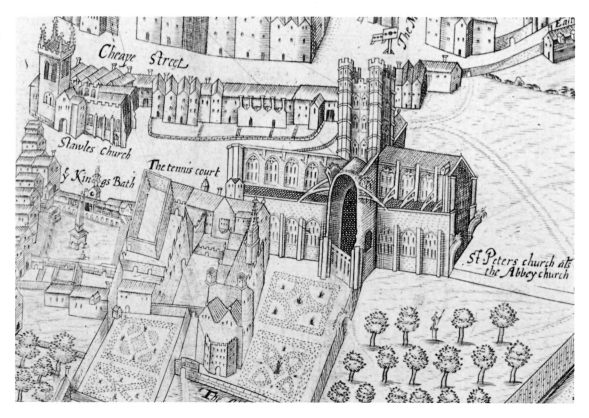

The earliest reliable images of Bath date to around 1600. The monastery, which had included the King's Bath within its precincts, was dissolved in 1539. The King's Bath now enjoyed greater public access from the yard in front of the new Abbey Church, seen here still under construction.

THE 17TH CENTURY SPA

Bladud, legendary founder of Bath, has presided over the hot springs in the King's Bath since the 17th century. The origins of the statue are unclear; it is possible that the head and body were brought together from different medieval statues elsewhere in the city.

Throughout the Middle Ages the life of Bath was dominated by the Abbey which occupied almost a quarter of the walled town and owned much of the land around. It was a time of stagnation but with the Reformation at the beginning of the sixteenth century things began to change and the small community whose livelihood had been based on the local wool trade looked to wider horizons.

With the power of the monasteries all but destroyed and their vast landholdings dispersed there was a new entrepreneurial spirit abroad in Bath. Monastic property, including the baths and the charitable hospitals in the south-west quarter of the town, passed to the civic authorities. The curative properties of the three springs, the King's Bath, the Cross Bath and the Hot Bath, were widely known and attracted hoards of the sick and needy – as one contemporary writer put it, there were 'many beggars in that place, some native there, others repairing thither from all parts of the land, the poor for alms, the pained for ease'.

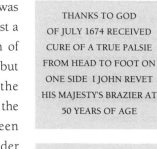

THANKS TO GOD OF JULY 1674 RECEIVED CURE OF A TRUE PALSIE FROM HEAD TO FOOT ON ONE SIDE I JOHN REVET HIS MAJESTY'S BRAZIER AT 50 YEARS OF AGE

BLADUD SON TO LUD HUDEBRAS THE EIGHTH KING OF THE BRITAINS FROM BRUTE, A GREAT PHILOSOPHER, AND MATHEMATITIAN: BRED AT ATHENS, AND RECORDED THE FIRST DISCOVERER, AND FOUNDER OF THESE BATHES, EIGHT HUNDRED SIXTY AND THREE YEARES BEFORE CHRIST, THAT IS TWO THOUSAND FIVE HUNDRED THIRTY FIVE YEARS SINCE ANNO DOMINI 1699

Of the bath of Baeth in the counte of Summersetshyre:

The casting of children out, before the dew tyme appoynted by nature.

The hardnes and bynding of the belly, when as a man can not go to the stool without Phisik.

The knobbes & hard lupes that ar made by the french pockes.

Wormes in the belly.

Barunnes of man or woman.

The vayn appetite of goyng to stoole, when a man can do nothing when he cummeth there.

Dr William Turner 1562

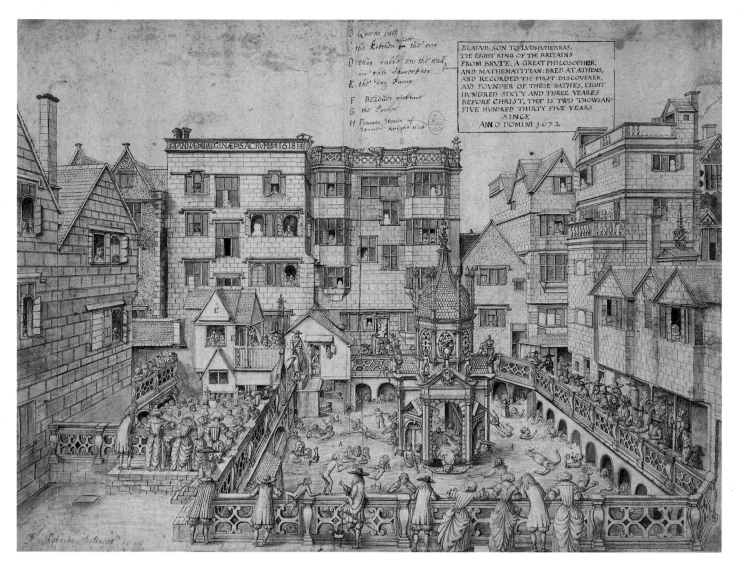

B Queens bath
C the Kittchen in the ...
D this table on the wall, in this showerbox...
E the Dry Pumie
F Bredas ...bath
G the Bortox
H Francis Stonor of Stonor knight 1624

BLADUD, SON TO LVDHVDEBRAS, THE EIGHT KING OF THE BRITAINS FROM BRVTE, A GREAT PHILOSOPHER, AND MATHEMATITIAN: BRED AT ATHENS, AND RECORDED THE FIRST DISCOVERER, AND FOVNDER OF THESE BATHES, EIGHT HVNDRED SIXTY AND THREE YEARES BEFORE CHRIST, THT IS TWO THOWSAND FIVE HVNDRED THIRTY FIVE YEARES SINCE ANNO DOMINI 1672.

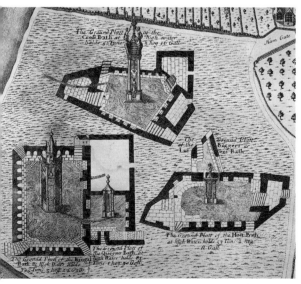

Gilmore's map of 1694 was perhaps the first tourist guide to the city. It provided a brief introduction and history, an illustrated guide to the accommodation, showed important buildings, gave a list of the taverns and, not least, portrayed detailed plans of the various baths.

Gradually the virtues of the waters became more widely known through the writings of men like Dr William Turner who in 1562 published a book about the spas of Europe, in it deliberately praising Bath to encourage his readers to travel to the town to take a cure. It was a beginning. Other works followed in quick succession and by the end of the century the benefits of Bath were recognised. The visit of Queen Anne of Denmark, wife of James I, in 1613 and 1615 sealed its destiny as a place of fashion.

The baths at this time were still in a rather squalid medieval state as Johnson's brilliant illustration shows. The arched recesses around the King's Bath had been built in the twelfth century but the elegant balustrade over which the onlookers lounge, was donated by Sir Francis Stonor in 1624 in recognition of the cure of his gout. The smaller bath to the south, later known as the Queen's Bath, had been added a century earlier in 1576. The huge ornamental feature in the centre of the King's Bath was acquired two years later. The transformation was beginning.

Before I took coach, I went to make a boy dive in the King's Bath – 1 shilling.

SAMUEL PEPY'S DIARY 1668

Thomas Johnson's evocative drawing of 1675 showing life in the King's and Queen's Baths. Bathing was a popular spectator sport with onlookers leering at the bodies in the water below. Naked children can be seen poised to dive for a coin tossed in by a well-dressed gentleman. The gabled buildings on the right were replaced by the first Pump Room in 1704-6.

THE PUMP ROOM 1706-1790

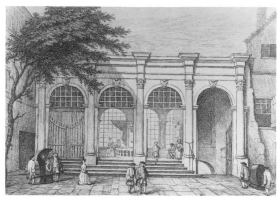

The Pump Room in 1739 as seen from the Abbey Church Yard. The right hand bay gave access down to the King's Bath changing rooms.

Richard 'Beau Nash', Master of Ceremonies in Bath from 1705-1761. While Nash presided over entertainments in the Pump Room, less dignified activities took place nearby. This bone enema nozzle would have been used as part of the Bath 'cure'.

The visit of Princess Anne in 1692 and her return as queen in 1702 and 1703 set the seal of aristocratic approval on Bath – where royalty led the aristocracy would follow. Bath was on the verge of becoming fashionable.

To cope with the new demands the city authorities began to initiate and later actively to support, a series of rebuilding schemes which were to transform the rather squalid little medieval town into one of Europe's most elegant cities in the course of the eighteenth century.

The first requirement was to make the approach to the King's Bath more agreeable by constructing a hall or Pump Room, where visitors could assemble to view the baths, drink the curative waters in comfort and prepare themselves to descend the slips – passageways leading down to the baths which also served as changing rooms. The first Pump Room was built by John Harvey in 1706 in the style of an orangery. It was a light airy structure of great charm well suited to the small throughput of visitors of the time, but as the fame of the spa became more widely known the original building had to be extended in the 1750s.

Longcase clock presented to the Corporation for the Pump Room by leading clockmaker Thomas Tompion in 1709. The gift included the sundial outside the window.

Fan of c.1737 showing the interior of the Pump Room. The pump for supplying spa water can be seen behind a rail; five musicians are playing in the gallery, the precursors of the Pump Room Trio.

The enlarged Pump Room 1764-5. The original orangery was extended by one bay and sported a more ornate cornice, decorated on the north side with stone urns. Access to the King's Bath was now possible from both the Abbey Church Yard and the passage beside the bath.

By the 1780s, when the popularity of Bath was nearing its peak the Corporation decided that the entire city centre had to be replanned and a far more spacious Pump Room constructed. Work began in 1786 when Thomas Baldwin built the colonnade between the Abbey Church Yard and Stall Street and two years later completed the New Private Baths to the south. Then in 1790 the foundation trenches for the new Pump Room were dug, bringing to light the steps of the Roman temple and a substantial part of the Gorgon's head pediment. It took six years before the Pump Room was finally opened to the public but by then the bubble of prosperity had burst. The war with France and the depression of 1793 brought building programmes to a halt in a flurry of bankruptcies. As the Pump Room opened its doors the great days of Bath were fast drawing to a close.

Thomas Rowlandson's satirical view of the King's Bath from his COMFORTS OF BATH (1798). His gout-ridden invalid can be seen struggling through the water with the aid of two sticks.

THE GRAND PUMP ROOM

The Grand Pump Room was opened by the Duchess of York on 28 December 1795. The building had been designed by the city architect Thomas Baldwin but Baldwin was also involved in several private schemes and when the economic depression of 1793 hit Bath he was declared bankrupt and had to resign. The building was completed by John Palmer but not, it seems, exactly to the original plans for there is evidence in the surviving foundations to suggest that Baldwin had intended the four-columned portico, now attached to the north front, to stand proud in the manner of a classical temple. Visually this would have undoubtedly been more imposing than the present arrangement. It was a strange coincidence that the very foundation trenches he dug unearthed parts of the original Roman temple of very similar style and proportions!

Inside, the elegant hall is still much as it was when first built. Water was pumped up to a fountain where a pumper served those who wished to drink it. Two large fireplaces warmed the cavernous space and musicians entertained the assembly from the western apse. Since it was customary to drink the prescribed number of glasses before breakfast the doors opened at 6 a.m. in summer and by 8 a.m. the room was thronged. 'There you see the highest quality and lowest trades-folk, jostling each other hail fellow-well-met' said a character in one of Tobias Smollett's novels written in 1771; and Jane

The interior of the Pump Room today is little altered from the original design. Despite being heavily furnished the room retains the calm classical elegance of the late 18th century. The tradition of refreshments and entertainment continues today.

Visitors to the Pump Room were expected to pay for the spa water they drank. The position of Pumper was let by the Corporation on an annual lease. The post was a lucrative one; by the end of the 18th century the lease was worth £800 per annum. Complaints were voiced that the new Pump Room lacked facilities for "when the waters begin to operate".

Austen, at the end of the century, describes in *Northanger Abbey* how one of her characters, after drinking his glass of water, joined friends to talk over the newspapers and the politics of the day while the ladies 'walked together, noticing every new face and almost every new bonnet in the room'. It was a place to linger in, to converse, to see and be seen.

This sparsely populated view of the Pump Room by J.C.Nattes (1804) shows the austerity of the interior. The visitors provided all the necessary diversion. Jane Austen came here to observe the company and its fashions.

Aquatint by David Cox (1820) (top left) showing a busy traffic of sedan chairs in the Abbey Church Yard carrying visitors to and from the Pump Room. Sedan chairs awaiting passengers are parked beneath the colonnade.

VICTORIAN DISCOVERIES

The great phase of building in Bath throughout the eighteenth century had demonstrated beyond doubt that remarkable Roman monuments lay beneath the town centre. In 1727 the gilded bronze head of Minerva had been found beneath Stall Street, in 1755 part of the eastern end of the baths was exposed in building work and in 1790 the foundation trenches for the Pump Room had unearthed a substantial part of the temple.

There matters rested until 1867 when work began on the Grand Pump Room Hotel on the west side of Stall Street. The foundation works were carefully observed by James Irvine, a clerk of works overseeing the restoration of the Abbey. He was a highly competent antiquarian who was able to record and recognise for what it was the platform upon which the temple was built, but his work went largely unnoticed at the time.

The real breakthough came in 1878 when the city surveyor and architect, Major Charles Davis, worried by a leak in the King's Bath, decided to explore the ground around it and in doing so found Roman remains. A year later he had taken up the floor and was astounding the archaeological world with finds dredged from the Roman reservoir beneath. After that there was no stopping him. In 1880-1 he had uncovered large parts of the Great Bath, encouraging the city authorities to buy up the properties above and demolish them so that the Roman bathing establishment could be uncovered. Economic necessity required that the western end was largely obscured beneath a new suite of spa facilities, but the Circular Bath and the Great Bath were open for all to see and remain a lasting monument to Davis's vision and persistence.

The present array of buildings including the Concert Room, now the Museum entrance hall, the colonnade around the Great Bath and the terrace with its statues above was completed by J.M. Brydon in the closing years of the century providing the city with a monument for which it is famed throughout the world.

Excavations beneath the Queen's Bath revealed a large circular pool in the Roman complex beneath. The Queen's Bath was completely demolished. The back of Bladud's niche in the King's Bath can be seen beyond.

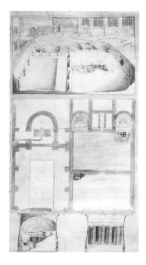

The first major discovery of the Roman Baths was made in 1755 and recorded by Bath artist William Hoare. His drawing of the eastern range of baths south of the Abbey was a clue that a major bathing establishment lay buried nearby. The large rectangular pool was suspected but unproven until the 1880s.

Major Davis's proposal to erect a new vault over the bath was passed over in favour of Brydon's open, more Italianate, scheme.

THE TWENTIETH CENTURY

The twentieth century began in Bath in a spirit of boisterous enthusiasm with the opening of the huge Empire Hotel – a vast pile which has since dominated the heart of the city and is only now beginning to be accepted as a building of some architectural merit. It was redundant almost before it was finished – the last defiant gesture of a town desperate to cling on to its past as one of the great spas of Europe.

The twentieth century has seen the life of Bath change out of all recognition. Gone were the days when fashionable society flocked to the city to take the waters. The best that a guide-book of 1920 could claim was that 'Bath has its value as a health resort, particularly to invalids in the winter time'. The Grand Pump Room Hotel, built with such enthusiasm in 1869, lasted barely 90 years before it was demolished to make way for shops and apartments, and the New Baths of the 1880s were swept away in the early 1970s. Manners and aspirations change and so must the city change with them.

Today's visitors come for different reasons. Bath is an architectural masterpiece – one of the most harmonious cities of the world. It is also a place with an awe-inspiring symbol of continuity – the spring – taking us back deep into prehistory. Wandering among the Georgian terraces or watching the spring cascade from the reservoir our senses cannot fail to be sharpened and our curiosity stirred. How different today's visitors are from their fellows 180 or 1800 years ago and yet like Priscus, the stone mason from Roman Gaul or Jane Austen, they too are drawn to Bath by the powerful fascination of the spring.

In the early 20th century spa water was aerated, bottled and widely distributed, using the name Sulis Water. The principal drawback of this operation was that the water lost its unique characteristic of warmth.

The New Private Baths, erected in 1889 over the Roman west baths, included a number of interesting treatments. The Four-Cell or Schnee Bath involved the use of electricity in conjunction with spa water. This patient, seen here around 1914, watches with concern as the nurse switches on the current.

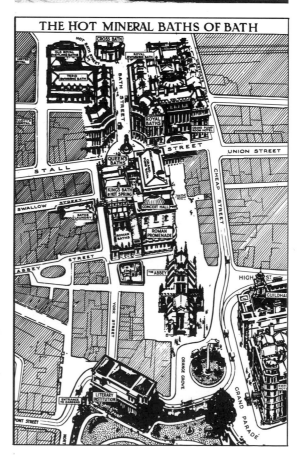

THE HOT MINERAL BATHS OF BATH

The Pump Room and Roman Baths were at the centre of an impressive swathe of buildings across the centre of Bath, offering medical treatment, accommodation and places of entertainment, worship and culture. This view of c.1920 was drawn to show off this range of facilities.

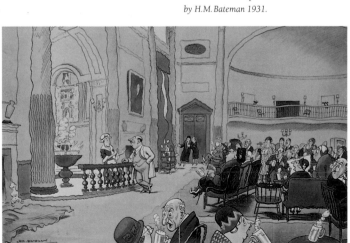

The terrace overlooking the Roman Baths, c.1914. Afternoon tea is being taken. The tranquility of this photo was soon to be shattered; during the Great War wounded servicemen were sent to Bath to drink the waters.

With so many pleasant and interesting reasons for visiting Bath, I may be forgiven for hoping that it may be long before I am compelled to come here for the sake of your healing waters. Happily, their virtues need no praise from me. They were well known to the Romans, but in our own day they have restored the health of thousands who were afflicted in the Great War. The human sympathy the citizens of Bath have always shown for the suffering is no less admirable than the lovely setting of the city, and the magnificent architecture which is the wonder of the world.

H.R.H. The Prince of Wales 1923

Fred Taylor's poster of 1926 portrays the Pump Room as a fashionable place to visit.

The Pump Room Orchestra playing in the Concert Room. Unfortunately, this room described by some as the New Kursaal had extremely poor acoustics and never succeeded as a concert venue. The Orchestra was disbanded in 1939.

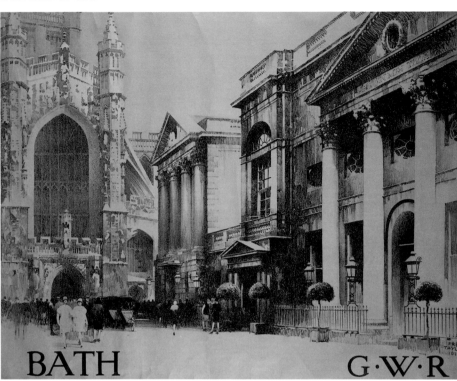

BATH

G·W·R

"The man who asked for a double scotch in the Grand Pump Room at Bath." by H.M. Bateman 1931.

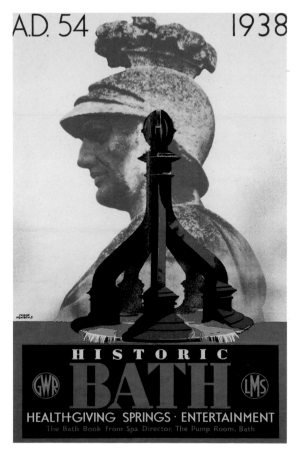

A.D. 54   1938

HISTORIC
GWR **BATH** LMS
HEALTH-GIVING SPRINGS · ENTERTAINMENT
The Bath Book from Spa Director. The Pump Room, Bath

Railway poster also used on the cover of City Guide Book.

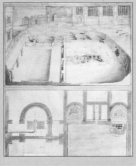

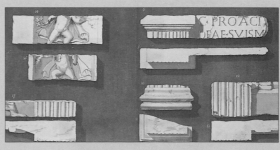

1727 discovery of Minerva's Head under Stall Street. West Baths hypocaust seen at the same time. Both recorded by Bernard Lens: the head was retained, the remains reburied.

1755 discovery of eastern baths during foundation digging for the Kingston Baths. Recorded by Bath artist William Hoare before being reburied.

1790 temple precinct observed during foundation digging for Pump Room; sculptured blocks from temple building and other structure recovered. In situ remains covered over by Pump Room.

1867 temple podium observed briefly before being covered by Grand Pump Room Hotel

1878-9 examination of Roman Sacred Spring and reservoir beneath King's Bath.

WHAT NEXT?

The temple precinct, now part of the Roman Baths Museum. The beams supporting the 18th century Pump Room can be seen above.

Archaeological work continues to seek new information about the buried past. In the city centre this is only possible when redevelopment takes place or opportunities arise beneath streets and standing buildings.

One of the great joys of archaeology is that discovery is never ending. The story of the Roman sanctuary and baths told in this book has been pieced together from fragments collected over the last 300 years – casual discoveries at first noted by local antiquaries, the eager uncoverings of the nineteenth century and the painstaking work of the Bath Archaeological Trust over the last thirty years, responding when necessary to the destruction of archaeological levels caused by redevelopment and, when time allows, carrying out programmes of carefully defined research into the city's development.

We have learnt a lot but there is so much more to learn. We are still largely ignorant of the state of the spring and its surroundings in the pre-Roman period. Where is the early Roman fort? The circular temple or *tholos* is still unlocated and the sanctuary must surely have been provided with a theatre about which we still know nothing. The Dark Ages in Bath are still dark in the extreme – we are not even sure where the Saxon church 'of marvellous workmanship' was. Even our knowledge of the layout of the Norman Abbey buildings is very incomplete. This is not a cry of despair or an admission of failure – it is an exciting agenda for the future.

1880-96 excavation of Great Bath, Circular Bath and parts of western range.

1923 Kingston Baths demolished and East Baths re-excavated.

1971 West Baths excavated in full.

1979-80 Roman Sacred Spring and reservoir re-excavated.

1981-83 Temple Precinct excavated beneath Pump Room.

47

"I'm afraid it will be very objectionable," I overheard a lady saying as she entered the Grand Pump Room, obviously for the first time in her life, intent on drinking some of the water.

"Not at all, madam," the uniformed attendant reassured her.

"It is a little warm and has a slight taste; that is all."

BATH, PAST AND PRESENT
H.M. Bateman 1939

This Guide is published by Bath Archaeological Trust and proceeds from its sale go towards further archaeological work in and around the city. The Trust is an independent charity which enjoys a close relationship with Bath and North East Somerset Council in their shared objective of researching, protecting and presenting to the public the historic environment of the district.

Written by Barry Cunliffe
Edited by Stephen Bird
Designed by Bridget Heal

Photography by Tim Mercer
Illustrations: Ivan Lapper (pages 4, 7, 13, 24, 28-29)
James Kingston Stewart (pages 2, 5, 7, 30)
Archive photography by Fotek

Other photographs by kind permission of:
Ancient Art & Architectural Collection (pages 8, 10)
Bath Central Library (pages 38, 39, 40, 42, 45)
British Library (pages 43, 46)
British Museum (pages 14, 15, 16, 24)
National Museum of Antiquities of Scotland (page 12)
National Portrait Gallery (pages 41, 43)
RIBA Library (page 31)
Sotheby's (page 24)
Stephen Bird (pages 5, 12)
Victoria Art Gallery (pages 19, 38, 39, 45, 46)

The assistance of the following is gratefully acknowledged:
Bath Central Library: Liz Bevan
Bath Archaeological Trust: Peter Davenport
Kenneth Pearson
Roman Baths Museum: Stephen Clews
Jane Bircher
Victoria Art Gallery: Susan Sloman

© Bath Archaeological Trust 1993
Published by Bath Archaeological Trust 1993
Origination by Adroit Photo Litho
Printed in England by Barwell Colour Print
ISBN 0 9506180 2 0

Front cover: *The Great Bath overlooked by Bath Abbey – one of the great urban landscapes of Britain.*

Back cover: *The multi-period King's Bath – site of the Roman Reservoir and Sacred Spring and heart of the spa from medieval times to the 20th century.*

Opposite: *The hot spring in the King's Bath, the phenomenon that since Stone Age times has drawn people to Bath.*